RAILWAYS

Rod Prince

Macdonald Educational

How to use this book

First, look at the contents page opposite. Read the chapter list to see if it includes the subject you want. The list tells you what each page is about. You can then find the page with the information you need.

If you want to know about one particular thing, look it up in the index on page 31. For example, if you want to know about signals, the index tells you that there is something about them on page 27. The index also lists the pictures in the book.

When you read this book, you will find some unusual words. The glossary on page 30 explains what they mean.

Series Editor
Margaret Conroy

Book Editors
John Morton and Polly Dunnett

Series Design
Robert Mathias/Anne Isseyegh

Book Design
Jane Robison

Production
Susan Mead

Picture Research
Kathleen Lockley

Factual Adviser
Basil Cooper

Reading Consultant
Amy Gibbs

Teacher Panel
Lynne McCoombe, Joanne Waterhouse, Catherine Daniel

Illustrations
Mike Atkinson 10-11, 17, 24-25
Clifford Meadway 18-19, 29
Gary Rees/Linda Rogers Associates 12-13, 14-15, 27
Kate Rogers 23

Photographs
Barnaby's Picture Library: 16T, 22B
Bettman Archive/B.B.C. Hulton Picture Library: 8
Nick Birch: 22-3
B.B.C. Hulton Picture Library: 16B, 20-1
British Railways Board: 26, 26-7
Museum of British Transport: 9
P.J. Howard/Millbrook House Collection: 21
Norwegian State Railways: 13
The Post Office: 6
S.N.C.F.: 15
Spectrum Colour Library: 10-11, 25, 28
TASS: 14-15
ZEFA: Cover, 7, 12

CONTENTS

PEOPLE AND GOODS

Who uses trains

There are railways in nearly every country in the world. Trains carry people and goods from place to place quickly and easily, and they also carry letters and parcels by day and by night. Trains which carry people are called passenger trains and freight trains carry goods.

Many people in the world travel by train every day and in some countries the train is the only way that most people can get around.

These postal workers are sorting out letters on a train. They put letters and packets for different towns or areas into different boxes. Letters posted during the day often travel by train overnight and arrive the next morning.

Even so, there are a lot of people who never need to travel by train at all. How often do you go anywhere by train?

People use trains for all kinds of different reasons. They use them to get to work or to go on business trips, to go to school, to visit friends and relations, or to go on holiday. You can use the railway to go to the shops, to a football match or to the seaside.

There are many things to do while you are on a train. You can read or play games or look out of the window. Students and business travellers often get on with some work. Trains which go a long way may have a restaurant where you can eat a meal or a buffet where you can buy snacks. What do you like to do on a train journey?

A crowded train in Indonesia. In some places the trains do not run very often. A lot of people use them, so they are usually very full.

How railways started

The first railways were built in Britain about 200 years ago. They carried coal, iron, stone and timber in wagons pulled by horses.

The first steam locomotive, or engine that pulls wagons along rails, was invented early in the nineteenth century, and in 1825 the first public steam railway opened. It ran between Stockton and Darlington in the north of England and, to begin with, only carried goods. A few years later railways began to carry passengers as well.

By 1850, there were railways all over Britain and, at the same time, they were spreading through Europe and across America.

A railway being built in America during the last century. The pieces of timber being laid out are called sleepers, and the rails will be laid on them. The steam engine at the back is burning wood, not coal.

Before railways were built, people had to travel by horse-drawn coach or wagon, or on foot. Roads were bad and in wet weather coaches often got stuck in the mud. Most goods were carried by boats, on canals or rivers. The coming of the railway made travelling much easier, and trains could carry heavy loads more quickly than canal boats.

Life changed in many ways after the railways were built. For the first time in history, ordinary people could travel long distances because journeys were quicker and cheaper than ever before. News and letters travelled faster by train. Even the food people ate changed, because trains could carry fish from the sea, and fresh milk from farms, straight to towns and cities.

These trains ran on the first railway in France which opened in 1829. It went from Lyon to Saint Etienne. The goods train in the top picture was horse-drawn, but the coal train at the bottom was heavier, and needed a steam engine to pull it.

Freight by rail

All sorts of things that we use every day come to us by train. For example, trains carry a lot of the food we eat, and our letters, parcels and newspapers. Freight trains carry coal and oil to factories and bring goods from factories to the places where they are needed.

Different kinds of goods need different kinds of wagon to carry them. Fish and meat, for example, need refrigerated wagons to keep them cold, and there are whole trains made up of special wagons that carry new cars from the factory. Next time you go by train, see how many different types of wagon you can spot.

Many freight trains are made up of flat wagons that carry big boxes, or containers, full of goods. Cranes can lift the containers off the wagons and put them straight on to a ship or lorry. This way containers can make long, complicated journeys without being unpacked.

1.

In some countries, there are more freight trains than passenger trains. For example, in Africa, most railways run between mining areas and sea-ports and carry things like copper and iron ore for sending abroad by ship. In huge countries like the United States or the Soviet Union, goods may need to travel thousands of kilometres. The railway is the best way to carry heavy loads over such long distances.

Different types of freight wagon:
1. **Container wagon**
2. **Gravel hopper**
3. **Chemical wagon**
4. **Cement carrier**
5. **Timber wagon**
6. **Refrigerated van**

Heavy freight trains need powerful engines to pull them. This one in the United States is hauled by three diesel engines joined together.

2.

3.

4.

5.

6.

Rail or road?

Trains are often more useful than cars. In poor countries, where roads are bad and hardly anyone has a car, the railway can be the only way to travel. Even in rich countries, where there are a lot of cars, many people can't drive and don't have cars. Often people who have cars choose to use the train instead if, for example, they want to travel into a busy city centre, where there is a lot of traffic, and parking is difficult.

One railway train can carry as many people as 200 cars, or as much freight as 25 lorries. Trains use less fuel than cars or lorries for each passenger or tonne of goods they carry.

bills and other expenses

building and mending trains

office work

This diagram shows how your fare is spent

Cars, vans and lorries are caught in this traffic jam in Munich, in West Germany. Trains run to a timetable, and do not get held up by traffic.

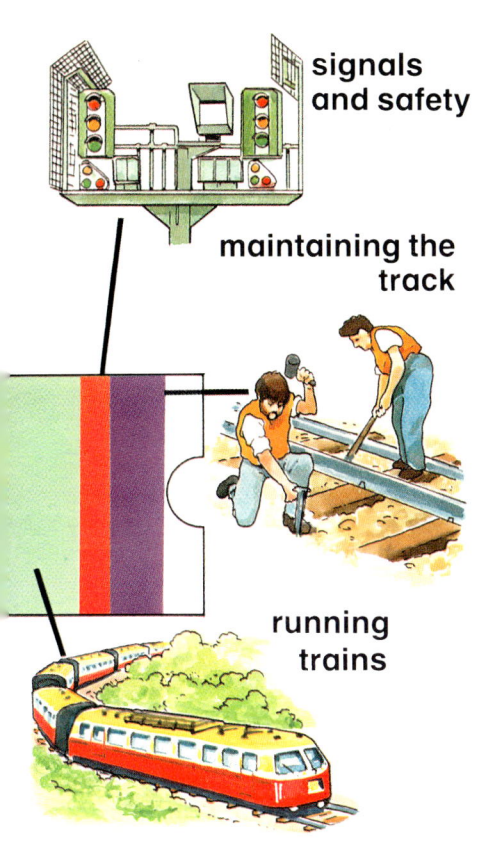

signals and safety

maintaining the track

running trains

Rail travel is faster and safer than road, and trains still run in bad weather when the roads are more dangerous.

But sometimes it is easier to travel by road. If you have a car, you can go where you like straight from home. You can put your luggage in the car instead of having to carry it to the railway station. Vans and lorries can deliver goods to your door. And cars, buses and lorries can get to places that are nowhere near a station.

Governments usually help pay the cost of running the railways. Without this help, railway companies would have to charge higher fares. But if the train is too expensive a lot of people and goods will go by road instead. In poor countries, people may not be able to travel at all.

Railways still run when snow and ice block the roads. This picture shows a snow-plough clearing a line in Norway.

13

GOING BY TRAIN

Main lines

The railway lines that connect big cities a long way apart are called main lines. On a main line you can catch an express train which travels fast and only stops at the biggest and most important stations. If you are only making a short trip, you usually catch a smaller, local train, which stops at every station.

Expresses and local, stopping trains often use separate tracks. The main line tracks are made as straight and level as possible so that express trains can run fast.

When railways first started, main line trains stopped quite often because the engines had to fill up with coal and water. But nowadays, diesel and electric engines can run long distances without stopping. Also, early trains had no refreshments or toilets on board. Now carriages are more comfortable and people can buy snacks and meals on the train.

International express trains run through more than one country. On some journeys in Europe you can go through five or six countries on the same train. But it can take several days to travel across just one very large country like Canada or Australia.

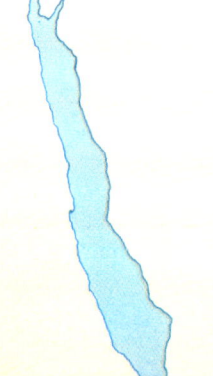

The Trans-Siberian is the longest railway in the world. It goes from Moscow to the Pacific Ocean, 8500 kilometres away. On fast trains, the journey takes five days.

An express train in the Ural Mountains in Russia. It is on the Soviet Union's most famous railway, the Trans-Siberian.

Sverdlovsk
Omsk
Novosibirsk
Tayshet
Bratsk
Irkutsk
Ulan Ude
Chita
Tynda
Komsomolsk
Khabarovsk
Vladivostok

These passengers on the French high-speed train, the TGV, are enjoying a meal in the restaurant car. You can also get snacks and drinks on the train.

Railways in cities

In the centres of big cities, the streets are often crowded with cars, so people use railways to get around quickly. Railways in towns are usually built underground to save space. The stations are close together and the trains run every few minutes. The trains don't have many seats, but they have room for a lot of people to stand. Some city railways connect with local railways that bring people in from their homes in the suburbs.

The first underground railway was opened in London in 1863. It was called the Metropolitan Railway and it ran just below street level.

Not all trains run over rails. The carriages of this train at Wuppertal in West Germany hang from an overhead line.

Underground railways were built because the streets in big cities were very crowded and the traffic made travelling slow. This is Fleet Street, in the centre of London, in the 1890s.

This cut-away picture of an underground station shows how different lines are connected by passages and stairways.

At first, the trains were pulled by steam engines, so it was very smoky in the tunnels. Nowadays, underground trains are electric and the tunnels are often much deeper.

Cities all over the world now have underground railways, and new ones are still being built. Hong Kong and Mexico City, for example, have new underground systems. Two older systems are the Paris Metro and the New York Subway.

The most modern underground railways are controlled by computer. The driver makes the doors open and close, and starts the train. After that, the computer controls how fast the train goes and when it stops. In Lille, in France, all the trains are automatic, and have no drivers.

entrance

ticket barrier

moving staircase

passage

platform

train

tunnel

17

Country railways

Country people in many parts of the world use railways to travel from their village to the nearest town. On market day, the train is full of people taking vegetables, fruit and animals to sell. They come back with things they need for their farms and houses.

Country railways often have a single track, except at places where trains need to pass. There may be only two or three trains a day, and they may have both passenger coaches and goods wagons. Trains on country railways often do not go very fast, and if you're late for a train the driver may wait for you. You may buy tickets on the train, instead of at a ticket office.

At old-fashioned level crossings, the railways have to pay someone to open and close the gates.

This railbus is like an ordinary bus, but it has steel wheels so that it can run on rails. It uses less fuel than a train.

In rich countries like Britain, France and the United States, many railways in country areas have been closed down, because most people now have cars and do not often need to use trains. It is expensive to keep country lines open, when few people use the train. Closed railway lines are sometimes made into long distance footpaths or nature reserves.

However, country towns and villages which still have railways often want to keep them. It is useful to have local trains which connect with main line services and many people prefer the train to a bus service, which is often slower and less reliable. So the railway companies are trying to find ways of making country lines cheaper to run. The illustrations on this page show two of their ideas.

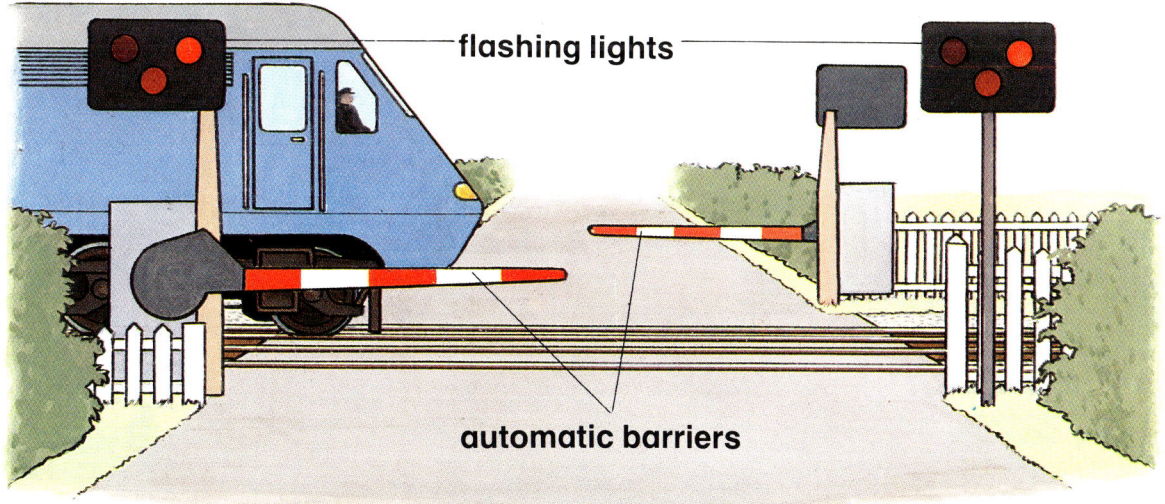

flashing lights

automatic barriers

New level crossings have barriers which close automatically when a train is coming. The lights warn the road traffic.

Railways for pleasure

Before railways were invented, only a few, rich people travelled for pleasure. Ordinary people did not have holidays and could not afford to travel around the country.

But as the railways spread, so did the idea of cheap day trips, or excursions. Seaside towns in Britain and other countries became popular places to go to by train. Later in the nineteenth century, factory workers started to get paid holidays and they spent them in seaside resorts. Towns like Brighton in the south of England and Calais in France grew fast, as more and more people had enough time and money for days out and holidays.

People now make a special trip to travel on a steam railway. There is always a crowd of admirers round the engine. This one is in Australia.

The railway also made it easy to travel from one country to another. Nowadays, of course, you can fly or drive to a different country for a holiday, but many people still go by train. Young people can get cheap rail tickets to visit several countries.

Railways themselves can be fun. Some seaside towns have railways running along the beach. In other places there are miniature railways where you can ride in open carriages. You can also visit model railways. In Switzerland you can travel on mountain railways, which climb thousands of metres to the mountain tops.

If you want to see what railways used to be like, why not visit a steam railway, where some of the old engines are still working?

Before many people had cars, almost everyone went on holiday by train. These people are waiting for a train to the seaside. It is 1922.

This Canadian train has a special observation car with windows in the roof. It runs through the Rocky Mountains, and the big windows give passengers an all-round view of the scenery.

Stations

A railway station may be just a platform with a passenger shelter on it. It may have only one person to sell and collect tickets as well as do all the other jobs. But a station can be much more than a place to catch trains. The biggest stations are busy and exciting places.

A station where different railway lines meet is called a junction. Passengers often change from one train to another at a junction.

The station at the end of the line is called a terminus. A big terminus may have more than twenty platforms and an indicator to tell you where to find your train.

These stalls on an Indian station sell all sorts of food, from an orange to a hot meal.

Some railway stations, like this one at Kuala Lumpur, in Malaysia, were built to look like palaces.

On a railway station you can see people who catch the same train every day, to and from work. They are often in a hurry, and don't stop to look around, but rush straight for their train. Other people may be going on holiday with all their luggage. There are people seeing friends off on journeys, or welcoming them back. But plenty of people use stations even if they are not going anywhere.

A big city station often has cafés, restaurants, shops and even a hotel. You can have your hair cut, have a bath or watch a film. There is a bank, post office and information office for travellers. Outside, there is room for taxis to pull up, and often a bus terminus and an underground station. Hundreds of people may work on a big station.

A busy scene at a big terminus. How many of these people are there to catch a train?

HOW RAILWAYS WORK

Steam, diesel or electric

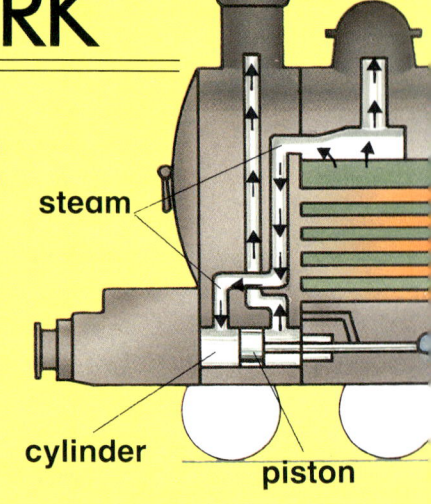

steam

cylinder

piston

Nowadays, trains in most parts of the world run on diesel or electric power. But steam was the main form of power for more than 100 years and, even now, steam engines still pull trains in China, India and a few other countries.

Electric trains were first made in Germany towards the end of the 19th century, and the first diesel train was tried out in Sweden in 1913. But electric and diesel trains did not replace steam until many years later.

Diesel engines make their own power as they go along, using oil as fuel. Electric trains run by picking up electric power from overhead wires or from a third rail at the side of the track. Underground trains usually get their power from a third rail.

Electric and diesel trains are faster and cleaner than steam. Electric trains are the cleanest of all, and they can run faster than diesel. They are also cheaper to run, but it costs a lot of money to put up the overhead wires that they need. Many railways use electric power for their busiest services and diesel for the others. But in some parts of the world, diesel engines pull all the trains.

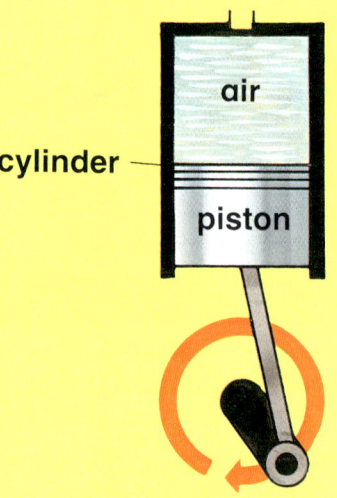

air

cylinder

piston

A diesel engine burns oil in the cylinders. The cylinder fills with air. As the piston pushes in, it compresses the air, which then gets very hot so that oil sprayed into the cylinder explodes.

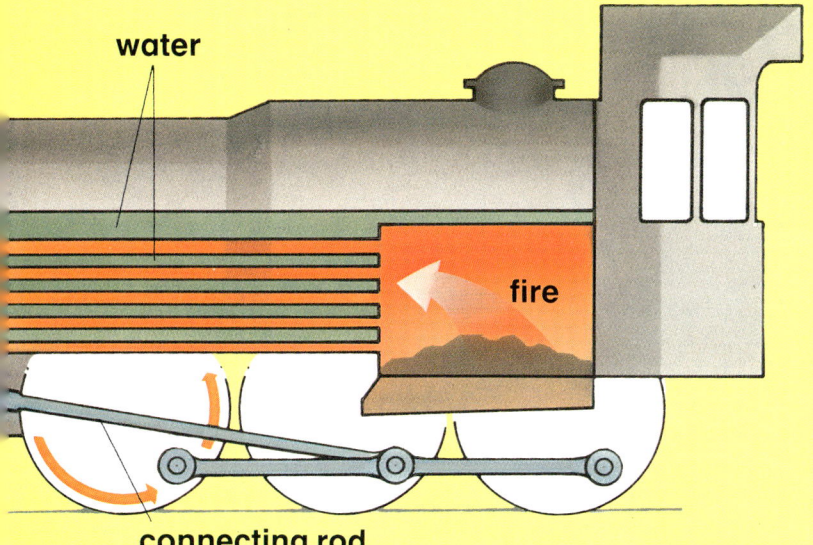

water

fire

connecting rod

The fire in a steam engine heats water in the boiler to make steam, which fills the cylinder. The steam in the cylinder pushes the piston backwards and forwards. The piston is connected to the wheels by a rod, and as it moves to and fro, it drives the wheels round.

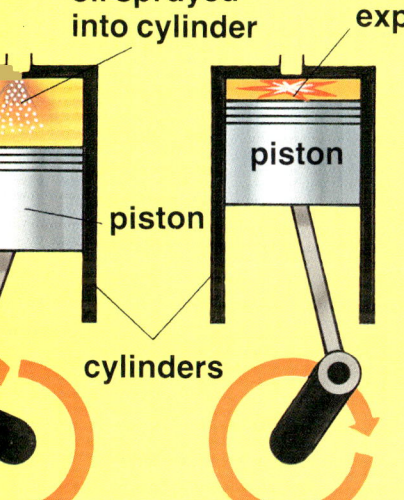

oil sprayed into cylinder

explosion

piston

piston

cylinders

The explosion pushes the piston out again. The piston is connected to the wheels and drives them round as it moves up and down.

An electric train in South Africa. The overhead wires carry the electricity.

Safety

Modern railways are a very safe way to travel. A lot of people work hard at keeping the track, signals and trains in good order and the railway companies also spend a lot of money on finding new ways to make trains even safer than they are now.

Everyone who works on the railway has to think about safety. There are also automatic safety systems to make sure accidents don't happen even when people make mistakes.

Train controllers at work in a signalling centre. The lights on the panel tell them where the trains are.

The driver's cab of a modern high-speed train. The big window gives a clear view of the line ahead and the signals.

The first railways were not very safe. One train followed another without anyone knowing how close they were. Engines had brakes, but coaches and wagons did not. Old fashioned rails could snap in two, and coaches made of wood got crushed easily in an accident. They could also catch fire. There were some serious accidents before things got better.

Nowadays, railway track is made of specially strengthened steel, and it is inspected often. Trains have powerful brakes and the coaches are made of steel or aluminium, both strong metals. Signals tell the drivers when to slow down or stop, and which route has been set for their train to follow at a junction. On many lines, the train's brakes go on automatically if a driver tries to go past a danger signal.

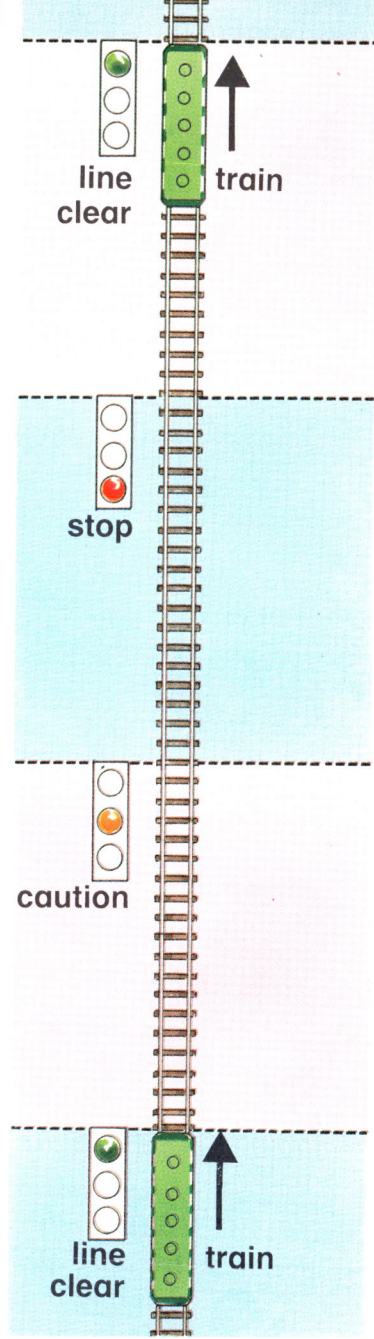

line clear

train

stop

caution

line clear

train

An automatic signalling system. The green light means the line is clear. As a train passes, the signal goes red. An amber light warns of a red light ahead.

New railways

Railways are still being built all over the world. Some of the new lines are in countries which have new industrial areas, such as Brazil, Australia and the Soviet Union. They need railways to carry machinery and goods to and from their new factories.

A double-decker train in Canada. It can carry many more passengers than an ordinary train. Double-decker trains are used on busy routes in several countries.

In Japan and France, the railways have become so busy that the railway companies have built new lines to take extra trains. Ordinary trains still run on the old track, and the new lines are specially made to carry very fast trains.

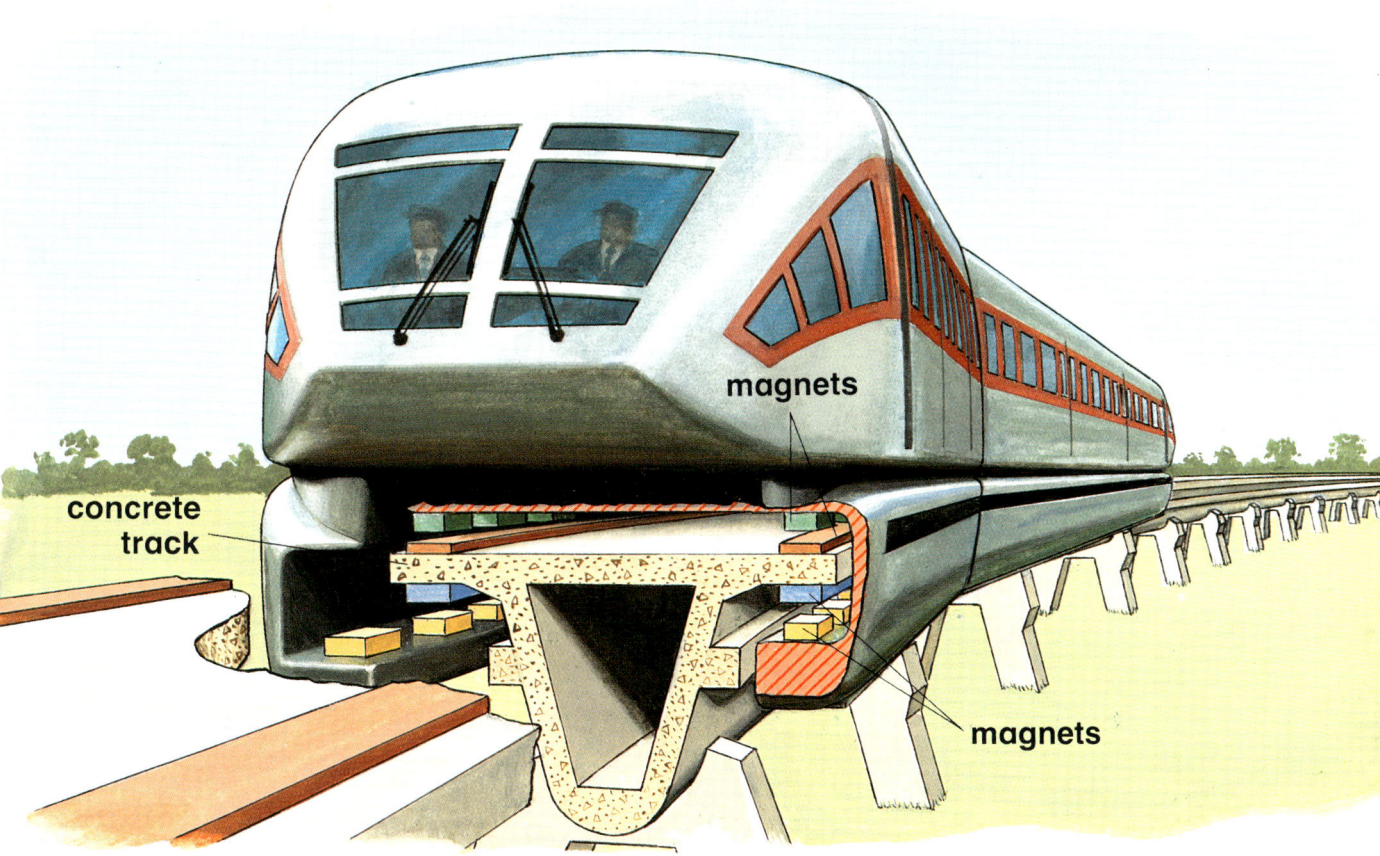

concrete track

magnets

magnets

The newest of these fast lines is the French high-speed railway. The train which runs on it is called the TGV, short for Train à Grande Vitesse, which is French for high-speed train.

Other railway companies are trying out different kinds of new train. One new train tilts over on curves, so that it doesn't have to slow down to go round corners. This means it can go fast on ordinary track and doesn't need a whole new line. Another is called the Maglev, and the picture on this page shows how it works.

Most of these new trains run with the help of computers. In the future, computers will be used more and more to help make trains run faster, as well as more cheaply and safely.

Maglev trains run on a concrete track with magnets in it. The magnets lift the train just clear of the track and also drive it along, so that it travels smoothly without touching the concrete. You might see a Maglev at an airport, being used to carry passengers to aeroplanes.

GLOSSARY, BOOKS TO READ

A glossary is a word list. This one explains unusual words that are used in this book.

Automatic Machines that work by themselves are automatic. Examples of things on railways that are often automatic are signals, doors, ticket machines, lifts, sometimes even whole trains.

Cylinder A tube-shaped box in an engine in which a piston slides to and fro. The piston is driven by the pressure of steam or gas.

Diesel engine An engine which burns oil in cylinders to make its own power. Large diesel engines make electricity which is used to drive the train.

Fare The money you pay for a ticket to travel by train.

Freight Goods of all kinds which are carried on trains are called freight.

Level crossing Place where a road crosses a railway line on the flat. It has gates or barriers to stop the road traffic when a train is coming.

Locomotive Engine which can move under its own power. Some passenger trains do not have a separate locomotive to pull the coaches. They have an electric or a diesel engine in the coaches themselves.

Maglev Train driven by magnets. It runs just above its track.

Piston Moving part inside a cylinder which drives an engine's wheels. The piston is pushed to and fro by the pressure of steam or gas in the cylinder.

Signals Signals tell train drivers when to stop and when it is safe to go on. Older signals have arms which move to different positions for 'stop' and 'go'. Modern signals use coloured lights: red for danger, orange for caution and green for a clear line ahead.

TGV Train à Grande Vitesse, which is French for high-speed train. The TGV runs on a special line, and new lines are now being built in several parts of France.

BOOKS TO READ

Most of these books are harder to read than this one. They all have lots of pictures.

Trains by Rixon Bucknall, Macdonald Educational, 1975
The Railway Age by L.W. Cowie, Macdonald, 1978
The Story of the Train by Patrick Whitehouse, W.H. Smith, 1984
Pictorial Encyclopaedia of Railways, by Hamilton Ellis, Hamlyn, 1983
The Guinness Book of Rail Facts and Feats by John Marshall, Guinness Superlatives, 1979